strategies for remote work business success

How to build and scale a business remotely, including tools, management practices, and maintaining productivity

hunter hazelton

life level up books, llc.

Strategies for Remote Work Business Success: How to build and scale a business remotely, including tools, management practices, and maintaining productivity

contents

BEFORE STARTING YOUR BUSINESS!

- CHOOSING A BUSINESS STRUCTURE
- REGISTERING A BUSINESS NAME
- BUSINESS TAX ID & LICENSES
- SETTING UP BUSINESS FINANCES
- GETTING BUSINESS INSURANCE
- PRODUCT DEVELOPMENT STRATEGIES
- MARKETING PLAN FOR STARTUPS
- SALES STRATEGIES FOR NEW BUSINESSES

HOW TO START YOUR

BUSINESS

Entrepreneurs Guide to Launching
Your Startup with Effective
Business Planning Strategies

HUNTER HAZELTON

embracing your remote business vision

. . .

IMAGINE STEPPING into a world where your office is anywhere you desire it to be: from the cozy corner of your favorite coffee shop to the serene backdrop of a beach house with the soothing sound of waves. This isn't a distant dream but the vibrant reality of embracing a **remote business model**. The allure of turning your entrepreneurial dreams into reality without the constraints of a physical office has never been more attainable or appealing, especially to the digital-savvy generation.

Discovering Your Remote Business Potential isn't just about breaking free from the 9-to-5 grind; it's about unlocking a universe of possibilities where scalability meets unprecedented flexibility. In this digital-first world, the unique value proposition of your

1

remote business isn't just a buzzword—it's your ticket to standing out in a crowded marketplace. Imagine the freedom to tap into talent from across the globe, harnessing the power of diversity to drive innovation and creativity in your business. It's not just about doing business differently; it's about redefining what it means to be a business in the 21st century.

Let's talk success stories, shall we? Picture a small tech startup that began in a cramped apartment in a bustling city, only to expand its operations across continents without opening a single additional office. Or consider the freelance graphic designer who transformed her passion into a thriving online business, collaborating with clients from Tokyo to Toronto, all from the comfort of her home studio. These aren't just feel-good tales; they're real-life examples of remote businesses thriving against the odds, proving that with the right approach, the world truly is your oyster.

But let's not sugarcoat it—embarking on this journey requires more than just a laptop and a dream. It demands a deep understanding of your market, a clear vision, and the grit to set and pursue ambitious goals. It's about crafting a business that reflects your values and vision, one that resonates with a global audience hungry for authenticity and innovation.

In **Chapter 1: Embracing Your Remote Business Vision**, we dive deep into the essence of what makes a remote business tick. From the initial spark of inspiration to the meticulous planning and resource allocation, every step is a building block towards creating a business that not only survives but thrives in the digital landscape. This chapter isn't just a roadmap; it's a manifesto for the modern entrepreneur ready to challenge the status quo and carve out their niche in the digital frontier.

So, as we embark on this journey together, remember: the path to remote business success is paved with challenges, but the rewards—freedom, flexibility, and the fulfillment of bringing your vision to life—are unparalleled. Let's turn the page and begin this adventure, shall we?

Diving into the world of remote business without understanding your market is like trying to navigate a ship in a storm without a compass—exciting but, let's face it, a bit reckless. **Understanding Your Market from a Distance** isn't just a fancy phrase we throw around to sound sophisticated. It's the secret sauce that can turn your remote business from a wild guess into a strategic masterpiece. And guess what? The digital age has handed us the tools to do just that, without having to leave our comfy home offices or favorite coffee spots.

Now, let's get real for a moment. Conducting **remote market research** and competitive analysis might sound like tasks reserved for those with fancy degrees or titles. But in reality, it's something any of us can do with a bit of internet savvy and the willingness to dive deep into the digital world. The internet is a treasure trove of information, with online data sources and virtual focus groups at our fingertips, ready to spill the secrets of customer needs and market trends. It's like having a crystal ball, but instead of vague predictions, you get actionable insights.

Imagine being able to tap into global conversations, understanding what makes your audience tick, and tailoring your business to meet their needs—without ever having to board a plane. Tools like social media analytics, online surveys, and keyword research can give you a glimpse into the minds of your potential customers, no matter where in the world they are. It's like being a digital Sherlock Holmes, piecing together clues to solve the mystery of market demand.

But here's where a pinch of humor comes in handy. Picture trying to use a virtual focus group to understand the needs of cat owners for your new line of pet products. You might end up with more videos of cats walking across keyboards than actionable feedback. It's a reminder that while digital tools are powerful, they also have their quirks. The key is to approach this task with a sense of humor and the understanding that not every piece of data will be a golden nugget of wisdom.

In the grand scheme of **Chapter 1: Embracing**

Your Remote Business Vision, understanding your market from a distance is like laying the foundation for your digital empire. It's about using the tools and resources available to not just guess what your customers want, but to know it, to anticipate it, and to meet them where they are. And let's not forget, it's about doing all this while possibly wearing pajamas, because who said market research can't be comfortable?

So, as we wrap up this segment, remember: the world of remote business is vast and full of potential. By leveraging digital tools to understand your market, you're not just guessing; you're strategically planning for success. And who knows? Maybe your remote business will be the next success story we talk about, inspiring a new generation of entrepreneurs to take the leap into the digital unknown. Let's turn that crystal ball into a roadmap and chart a course for success, shall we?

In a world where the only constant is change, setting goals for your remote business is akin to plotting a course through the vast and unpredictable digital ocean. **Goal Setting for Remote Success** isn't just about scribbling down lofty aspirations on a piece of paper; it's about charting a strategic path that is both ambitious and adaptable, ensuring your remote venture not only survives but thrives in the ever-evolving digital landscape.

Let's break it down, shall we? Establishing **SMART goals**—that's Specific, Measurable, Achievable, Relevant, and Time-bound, for those who haven't had their morning coffee yet—isn't a new concept. However, when it comes to the remote work arena, these goals take on a new level of significance. Imagine trying to coordinate a team spread across different time zones, cultures, and coffee preferences. Your goals need to be crystal clear to ensure everyone is rowing in the same direction, even if some are doing so in their pajamas.

But here's the kicker: while being specific is crucial, flexibility and adaptability are your best friends in the remote world. It's like planning a road trip with the understanding that some roads might be closed, and you might have to take a detour through some scenic (read: unexpected) routes. For remote teams, the ability to pivot and adapt goals as circumstances change is not just a nice-to-have; it's a must-have. After all, who hasn't had to suddenly recalibrate their plans because a team member decided to go on a digital nomad adventure in a timezone that's 12 hours ahead?

Incorporating flexibility into your goal setting means acknowledging that the path to achieving them might look different than initially planned. It's about setting up regular check-ins and feedback loops, ensuring that as the remote work landscape shifts, your goals can shift with it, without losing sight of the ultimate destination. It's a delicate balance between having a clear direction and being open to the journey's twists and turns.

Remember that goal setting for remote success is not just a one-time activity; it's an ongoing process of refinement and adaptation. It's about being as dynamic and fluid as the digital world we operate in, ready to seize opportunities or tackle challenges that come our way.

So, as you jot down your SMART goals, remember to infuse them with a dose of flexibility and adaptability. After all, in the remote business world, the ability to pivot might just be the secret ingredient to your success. And who knows? The detours you take might lead to discoveries and achievements far beyond what you initially imagined. Let's embrace the journey, shall we?

In today's fast-paced digital world, mastering **Resource Planning in a Virtual Environment** is not just an advantage; it's a necessity for anyone looking to elevate their business beyond the traditional confines of office walls. This strategic approach is the linchpin for transforming your entrepreneurial vision into a thriving digital reality, enabling you to harness the full potential of both digital tools and human creativity. As we embark on this exploration, let's address the three pivotal concerns that are likely at the forefront of your mind: identifying essential resources, fostering a cohesive virtual team, and mastering the art of resource allocation.

Firstly, the question of **identifying essential resources** for remote operations often looms large. The digital landscape offers a plethora of tools designed to streamline communication, project management, and collaboration. However, the trick lies not in amassing a vast arsenal of tools but in selecting those that best fit your team's unique workflow and objectives. For instance, while **Slack** has become synonymous with team communication, exploring lesser-known tools like **Twist** can offer a more structured, thread-based approach to conversations, reducing the noise and distractions commonly associated with instant messaging platforms.

Building a **cohesive virtual team** is another area ripe with challenges and opportunities. The key here is not just about finding individuals with the right skill set but also about nurturing a culture of open communication, trust, and mutual respect. Regular virtual meetups and team-building activities are essential, but consider going a step further by implementing a 'virtual open door' policy through tools like **Calendly** integrated with **Zoom**, allowing team members to schedule one-on-one chats with you or other team leaders, fostering a culture of accessibility and support.

When it comes to **resource allocation**, the complexity of balancing project demands with team capacity can seem daunting. Utilizing project management tools like **Asana** or **Monday.com** provides a visual overview of who's working on what and by when. Yet, diving deeper into analytics with tools like **Jira** for agile teams can offer insights into team performance and workload distribution, enabling more informed decisions that ensure projects stay on track without overburdening your team.

As we navigate through, it becomes evident that the journey from conceptualizing to actualizing a remote business model is both challenging and exhilarating. It's a journey that demands not just a reevaluation of how we work but a complete overhaul of traditional business paradigms. This chapter, therefore, is not merely a guide but a call to action for modern entrepreneurs to embrace the digital revolution with open arms and minds.

In conclusion, the essence of resource planning in a virtual environment transcends the mere selection of tools and team members; it's about creating a dynamic ecosystem where innovation, collaboration, and productivity flourish. By addressing these critical areas with a strategic mindset and a dash of creativity, you're not just setting the stage for your business to survive in the digital age—you're ensuring it thrives. So, as we turn the page on traditional business models, let's step confidently into the digital unknown, armed with the knowledge and tools to navigate the future of work.

––––––

Discovering Your Remote Business Potential

EMBRACE THE DIGITAL-FIRST APPROACH: Recognize the unique value proposition of your remote business as a means to differentiate in a crowded marketplace. Leverage global talent and embrace diversity to fuel innovation.

Success Stories as Inspiration: Draw motivation from real-life examples of remote businesses that have scaled globally without the need for physical expansion, illustrating the viability and dynamism of remote models.

Understanding Your Market from a Distance

Leverage Digital Tools for Market Research: Utilize social media analytics, online surveys, and keyword research to gain insights into customer needs and market trends, enabling data-driven decision-making.

Maintain a Sense of Humor and Perspective: While digital tools offer invaluable insights, approach the data with a critical eye and a readiness to adapt strategies based on actionable feedback.

Goal Setting for Remote Success

Establish SMART Goals: Define clear, measurable, and achievable objectives that are relevant to your remote business model and bound by realistic timelines.

Incorporate Flexibility and Adaptability: Recognize the need for goals to evolve in response to the dynamic remote work environment, ensuring your business remains responsive and resilient.

Mastering Resource Planning in a Virtual Environment

Identify Essential Digital Tools: Select tools that align with your team's workflow and business objectives, focusing on those that enhance communication, project management, and collaboration.

Build a Cohesive Virtual Team: Foster a culture of openness, trust, and mutual respect, utilizing digital platforms to maintain regular communication and encourage team engagement.

Strategize Resource Allocation: Use project management software to balance project demands with team capacity, employing analytics to optimize workload distribution and team performance.

building your remote brand identity

. . .

IN THE DIGITAL AGE, where every brand is vying for attention, **Remote Brand Storytelling** emerges as the secret sauce to captivate and connect with a global audience. This isn't about bombarding your followers with sales pitches; it's about weaving a narrative that resonates on a personal level, turning viewers into loyal advocates for your brand. As we delve into the art of **Building Your Remote Brand Identity**, it's crucial to understand that storytelling is not just a marketing tactic; it's the heartbeat of your brand, pulsating through every tweet, post, and video shared across the digital landscape.

One of the first hurdles you might encounter is the challenge of crafting stories that not only capture attention but also embody the essence of your brand.

The key? Authenticity. In a world where consumers are bombarded with content, genuine stories stand out. It's not about creating a perfect image but sharing the real journey, the ups and downs, and the lessons learned along the way. For instance, consider how brands like **Patagonia** share their commitment to sustainability not just through product design but in stories that highlight their environmental initiatives. This approach not only informs but inspires action, creating a deeper connection with their audience.

Another pressing question is how to effectively utilize digital platforms to amplify your brand's mission and impact. The digital realm offers a plethora of channels, each with its unique strengths and audience. The trick lies in choosing the right platforms and tailoring your content to fit. Instagram and TikTok, with their visual-centric nature, are perfect for behind-the-scenes peeks and short, impactful stories. In contrast, LinkedIn offers a space for more in-depth discussions and thought leadership pieces. Leveraging tools like **Canva** for eye-catching graphics or **Buffer** for scheduling posts across platforms can streamline this process, ensuring your story reaches the right people at the right time.

Engaging your audience in your brand's narrative is another critical aspect of remote storytelling. It's not just about broadcasting your story; it's about creating a dialogue. Encourage feedback, share user-generated content, and let your audience know their voices are heard. This two-way communication not only enriches your brand's narrative but also fosters a sense of community. Platforms like **Twitter** and **Facebook** are ideal for sparking conversations, while **Instagram Stories** and **Polls** can provide immediate insights into your audience's preferences and opinions.

As we navigate through **Building Your Remote Brand Identity**, remember that remote brand story-telling is an ongoing journey, not a destination. It's about continuously evolving your narrative, experimenting with new formats, and engaging with your audience in meaningful ways. This chapter is not just a guide but an invitation to explore the limitless possibilities of storytelling in the digital age.

Remote Brand Storytelling is a powerful tool in the arsenal of any brand looking to make a mark in the digital world. By focusing on authenticity, strategically utilizing digital platforms, and fostering audience engagement, you can create a brand identity that resonates deeply with your target demographic. So, let's embrace the art of storytelling, and transform the way we connect with our global audience, one story at a time.

In the sprawling digital marketplace, where every pixel counts, **Visual Identity for Online Presence** emerges as a critical beacon for businesses aiming to carve out their niche. This isn't just about having a logo or a color scheme; it's about creating a visual language that speaks directly to the hearts and minds of your audience, making your brand unforgettable in the vast sea of online content. As we venture deeper into **Building Your Remote Brand Identity**, it becomes evident that establishing a strong visual identity is not merely an aesthetic choice but a strategic one, especially for engaging with a younger, visually literate audience.

The first question that often arises is, "How can I design a visual identity that truly stands out?" The answer lies in understanding the unique story your brand seeks to tell. Just as **Patagonia** uses its visual identity to emphasize its commitment to sustainability, your brand should use its visual elements to reflect its core values and mission. This means going beyond generic templates to craft bespoke visuals that capture your brand's essence. Tools like **Adobe Creative Cloud** offer a suite of applications for those ready to dive deep into custom design, while **Canva** provides user-friendly options for those at the beginning of their design journey.

Navigating the digital platforms to share your brand's visual elements effectively is another hurdle. Each platform, from **Instagram** to **LinkedIn**, offers unique opportunities to showcase your visual identity. The trick is not just to be present but to be visually consistent across these channels. This consistency helps in building brand recognition. Utilizing a platform like **Buffer** or **Hootsuite** for scheduling posts can help maintain this consistency, ensuring that your visual identity is communicated clearly, no matter where your audience encounters your brand.

Engagement is the third pillar of building a strong visual identity online. It's not enough to just broadcast your visuals; you need to create opportunities for interaction. This could mean designing interactive infographics, engaging Instagram stories, or visually appealing polls that invite your audience to participate in the narrative you're creating. Tools like **Interactive Content** by **Outgrow** allow you to create quizzes, polls, and interactive infographics that can make your visual content not just seen but experienced.

As we navigate the intricacies of **Building Your Remote Brand Identity**, it's clear that **Visual Identity for Online Presence** is more than just a layer of polish on your brand; it's a fundamental component of how your brand communicates and connects with its audience. By focusing on authenticity, strategic platform use, and audience engagement, you can create a visual identity that not only stands out but also resonates deeply with your target demographic.

The journey to crafting a compelling visual identity in the digital realm is both an art and a science. It requires a blend of creativity, strategic thinking, and a deep understanding of the platforms where your audience lives. By addressing these critical areas with intention and innovation, you're not just creating a visual identity; you're building a visual legacy that can carry your brand forward in the digital age. So, let's embrace the challenge, armed with the right tools and a vision for the future, ready to make our mark one pixel at a time.

In today's digital cacophony, mastering the **Voice and Tone in Digital Communication** is akin to finding the perfect pitch in a symphony, crucial for brands aiming to harmonize with their audience's expectations and emotions. As we delve into **Building Your Remote Brand Identity**, it becomes clear that the voice you choose and the tone you adopt are not mere details but pivotal elements that can significantly influence how your message is received and perceived by a global audience. This strategic alignment of voice and tone is essential, especially when engaging with a demographic that values authenticity and connection over mere aesthetics.

One of the foremost questions that arise is, "How can I ensure my brand's voice remains consistent across all digital platforms?" Consistency in voice does not mean monotony; rather, it's about maintaining a recognizable personality across various channels. This consistency can be achieved by developing a comprehensive brand voice guideline that encapsulates your brand's ethos, mission, and values, ensuring that every piece of content, whether a tweet, blog post, or video script, reflects these core elements. Tools like **Grammarly** and **Hemingway Editor** can aid in maintaining this consistency, offering real-time suggestions to align your content with your established voice and tone guidelines.

Another pressing concern is, "How can I adapt my tone to fit different digital platforms without losing my brand's identity?" The digital landscape is vast, with each platform catering to a unique audience demographic and expectation. The key lies in understanding the nuances of each platform and adjusting your tone accordingly without diluting your brand's voice. For instance, LinkedIn demands a more professional and informative tone, while Instagram allows for a casual and visually engaging approach. Utilizing platforms like **CoSchedule's Headline Analyzer** can help tailor your message's tone to suit the platform while keeping your brand's voice intact.

Engagement is the cornerstone of effective digital communication. "How can I use my brand's voice and tone to foster genuine engagement with my audience?"

Engagement goes beyond mere likes and shares; it's about creating a dialogue. Your brand's voice should invite conversation, and your tone should make your audience feel valued and heard. Implementing interactive content, such as polls on Instagram Stories or Q&A sessions on Twitter, can encourage this dialogue, making your audience an active participant in your brand's narrative. Tools like **BuzzSumo** can provide insights into what content resonates most with your audience, helping you fine-tune your voice and tone for maximum engagement.

As we navigate the complexities of **Building Your Remote Brand Identity**, it's evident that **Voice and Tone in Digital Communication** are not just about how you say things but about how your message aligns with your audience's expectations and your brand's identity. By addressing these critical aspects with thoughtfulness and strategic planning, you can ensure that your brand not only speaks but sings, resonating deeply with your target demographic.

Crafting a voice and tone that resonate across digital platforms is an art that requires patience, experimentation, and a deep understanding of your audience. By focusing on consistency, adaptability, and engagement, you can ensure that your brand's voice is not just heard but listened to, creating a lasting impact in the digital realm. Let this be your guide as you sculpt your brand's digital identity, one word at a time, ensuring that every message you send out into the digital ether not only reaches its destination but also leaves a mark.

In the vast expanse of the digital world, where brands jostle for space and attention, **Brand Consistency Across Remote Channels** emerges as the linchpin for businesses aiming to carve a distinct identity. This isn't merely about plastering your logo across various platforms; it's about weaving a cohesive narrative that resonates uniformly, regardless of where your audience encounters your brand. As we delve deeper into the nuances of **Building Your Remote Brand Identity**, it becomes evident that ensuring a seamless brand representation online is not just beneficial—it's essential.

One might wonder, "How can I achieve a consistent brand presence across diverse digital landscapes?" The cornerstone of this endeavor is a robust brand guideline that transcends mere color palettes and fonts. It encompasses your brand's ethos, voice, and the emotional undertones of your messaging. Tools like **Adobe Spark** and **Canva** offer the versatility to create visually cohesive content, ensuring that every post, tweet, or update reinforces your brand's core identity.

Navigating through the maze of digital platforms,

each with its unique audience and content style, poses another challenge. "How do I maintain brand consistency while adapting to different platforms?" The answer lies in the strategic adaptation of your core message. Whether it's the professional confines of LinkedIn or the casual realms of Instagram, your brand's essence should remain unmistakable. Utilizing scheduling tools like **Buffer** or **Hootsuite** not only aids in maintaining a consistent posting schedule but also ensures that your messaging is tailored yet coherent, providing a unified brand experience.

Engagement—the lifeblood of digital brand presence—raises a pivotal question: "How can I use brand consistency to enhance engagement across channels?" Engagement thrives on familiarity and trust, which are byproducts of consistency. By employing interactive tools such as **Outgrow**, brands can create engaging, brand-aligned content that invites participation, fostering a community around your brand. Moreover, analytics tools like **Google Analytics** allow you to gauge the effectiveness of your brand consistency strategies, offering insights to fine-tune your approach.

As we chart the course through **Building Your Remote Brand Identity**, it's clear that **Brand Consistency Across Remote Channels** is not just about visual or verbal uniformity; it's about crafting a consistent brand experience that engenders trust and loyalty. By leveraging the right tools and strategies, you can ensure that your brand not only stands out but also stands for something meaningful, regardless of where or how your audience interacts with it.

In the digital marketing industry, where trends evolve at breakneck speed, maintaining brand consistency is akin to navigating a ship through turbulent waters. Yet, it's this consistency that acts as the beacon for your audience, guiding them back to your brand, time and again. As we conclude this exploration, remember that brand consistency is not a set-it-and-forget-it task but a dynamic, ongoing process. Embrace the latest technologies, like AI-driven content creation tools, to keep your brand's voice and tone consistent yet fresh. This forward-looking approach ensures that your brand not only resonates with today's audience but is also primed to captivate the digital denizens of tomorrow.

Crafting Your Narrative with Remote Brand Storytelling

EMBRACE AUTHENTICITY: Share your brand's true journey, including the highs and lows, to stand out in a content-saturated digital world. Authentic stories foster a deeper connection with your audience.

Strategically Utilize Digital Platforms: Tailor your storytelling to fit the unique strengths and audience of each platform, using tools like Canva for visuals and Buffer for post scheduling to maintain a cohesive narrative across channels.

Foster Audience Engagement: Create a dialogue around your brand's story, encouraging feedback and sharing user-generated content to build a community of brand advocates.

Establishing a Visual Identity for Online Presence

Design a Unique Visual Language: Reflect your brand's core values and mission through bespoke visuals, utilizing Adobe Creative Cloud for custom designs and Canva for accessible graphic creation.

Ensure Visual Consistency Across Channels: Use scheduling tools like Hootsuite to maintain a coherent visual presence, reinforcing brand recognition and loyalty.

Engage Through Interactive Visuals: Employ tools like Outgrow to create interactive content, making your visual identity not just seen but experienced.

Mastering Voice and Tone in Digital Communication

Develop a Comprehensive Brand Voice Guideline: Ensure consistency in your brand's personality across all content, with Grammarly and Hemingway Editor aiding in aligning your messaging with your brand voice.

Adapt Tone for Different Platforms: Customize your tone to match the expectations of each digital platform, maintaining your brand's identity while resonating with diverse audiences.

Use Engagement to Refine Voice and Tone: Implement interactive content to foster dialogue, using insights from tools like BuzzSumo to align your communication style with audience preferences.

Achieving Brand Consistency Across Remote Channels

Create Robust Brand Guidelines: Beyond visuals, define the ethos, voice, and messaging of your brand, ensuring every digital interaction reflects your brand's identity.

Tailor Messaging for Platform-Specific Audiences: While maintaining a unified brand experience, adapt your core message for the nuances of each platform, ensuring consistency and engagement.

Leverage Analytics for Strategic Insights: Utilize Google Analytics to measure the impact of your consistency efforts, allowing for data-driven adjustments to enhance brand resonance.

In synthesizing these strategies, it's evident that building your remote brand identity is an ongoing, dynamic process that demands creativity, strategic thinking, and a deep understanding of digital platforms and audience engagement. By weaving authenticity into your storytelling, crafting a distinctive visual identity, maintaining a consistent voice and tone, and ensuring brand consistency across channels, you set the stage for a brand that not only captures attention but also cultivates loyalty and advocacy.

As you move forward, remember that the digital landscape is ever-evolving. Stay adaptable, embrace innovation, and continuously seek to understand and engage your audience in meaningful ways. Your brand's identity is not just a facet of your business—it's the soul of your connection with the global community. Let this guide be your compass as you navigate the vast digital expanse, building a brand identity that resonates, engages, and endures.

online presence and digital tools for remote work

. . .

IN A WORLD where the line between work and life blurs seamlessly, **Website Essentials for Remote Businesses** stand as the cornerstone of virtual success. Imagine crafting a digital haven that not only showcases your brand but also caters effortlessly to the dynamic needs of remote work and its clientele. This isn't about slapping together a few web pages; it's about creating a virtual ecosystem that supports, engages, and transacts with a global audience from anywhere, at any time.

Why does your website need to scream 'remote-friendly'? In a world where coffee shops can double as boardrooms, your website must be more than just visually appealing. It needs to be a Swiss Army knife—equipped with tools and features that make remote interactions as smooth as silk. Think **live chat functions** for real-time communication, **intuitive navigation** for ease of use, and **responsive design** that ensures your site looks great on a laptop or a smartphone screen. These aren't just nice-to-haves; they're non-negotiables for capturing and retaining a digitally savvy audience.

But how do you keep your remote audience engaged? It's simple: **Content is king, but engagement is queen.** Your website should be a treasure trove of interactive content, from blogs that spark conversations to videos that tell your brand's story in vivid color. And let's not forget the power of **social proof**—customer testimonials, case studies, and reviews that build trust and credibility without a handshake in sight.

And the million-dollar question: How do you turn virtual foot traffic into transactions? Here's where the magic of **seamless integration** comes into play. Incorporate e-commerce functionalities, secure payment gateways, and clear calls-to-action (CTAs) that guide your visitors from browsing to buying without breaking a sweat. Tools like **Shopify** or **WooCommerce** can transform your site from a digital brochure into a bustling marketplace.

As we navigate through **Chapter 3: Online Presence and Digital Tools for Remote Work**, remember that your website is more than just a digital business card. It's a living, breathing entity that reflects the essence of your remote brand. By focusing on these website essentials, you're not just building an online presence; you're crafting a digital lifeline that connects your brand to the world.

Let's not just think outside the box. Let's forget the box ever existed. Your website is your digital realm, a place where boundaries are limitless, and opportunities are just a click away. With the right tools, strategies, and a sprinkle of creativity, you can create a website that not only stands out in the digital expanse but also becomes a beacon for remote work enthusiasts and clients alike.

The selection of your digital tools becomes not just a matter of preference but a cornerstone of operational success. **Selecting Digital Tools for Remote Efficiency** is akin to equipping your virtual office with the best possible resources to ensure productivity and collaboration soar, regardless of geographical boundaries. This critical decision-making process can make or break the fluidity and effectiveness of remote operations, highlighting its paramount importance to entrepreneurs and remote teams alike.

Why is choosing the right digital tools so crucial for remote businesses? In a world where remote work is becoming the norm rather than the exception, the digital tools you choose are the lifelines of your business operations. They determine how effectively your team communicates, collaborates, and stays productive in a virtual environment. Selecting the right tools means ensuring that your team can work seamlessly, without the constraints of physical office space, thereby enhancing efficiency and maintaining a competitive edge in the digital marketplace.

How do you evaluate the myriad of digital tools available to find the best fit for your remote business? It's not about picking the most popular or the most feature-rich tool but finding the one that aligns perfectly with your business's unique needs and work processes. Criteria for selection should include ease of use, integration capabilities with other tools you're already using, scalability to grow with your business, and, importantly, security features to protect your data and your clients' information. Tools like **Trello** for project management, **Slack** for communication, and **Zoom** for video conferencing have become staples for many, but don't overlook niche tools that might offer unique advantages specific to your business needs.

What are some lesser-known digital tools that can significantly enhance remote work productivity and collaboration? Beyond the widely recognized giants, tools like **Asana** offer nuanced project tracking with a focus on tasks and milestones, while **Notion** provides an all-in-one workspace for notes, tasks, databases, and wikis. For team collaboration, **Miro** offers an online collaborative whiteboard platform that enables distributed teams to work effectively together, through brainstorming sessions and project planning. Meanwhile, **Airtable** combines the simplicity of a spreadsheet with the complexity of a database, perfect for managing projects, customers, and ideas.

The digital tools you select are not just about managing tasks; they're about fostering a culture of collaboration, efficiency, and innovation in a remote work setting. By carefully considering your options and selecting tools that align with your business's specific needs, you can create a robust digital ecosystem that supports your team's best work, no matter where they log in from.

In the journey of remote work, the tools you choose are your allies in navigating the digital expanse. They are the building blocks of a productive, connected, and efficient remote work environment. As you explore the vast array of digital tools available, remember that the goal is not to amass a collection of the latest gadgets and apps but to curate a toolkit that brings out the best in your team and your business. Let this exploration be guided by the unique demands and dynamics of your remote operations, ensuring that each tool you select is a step toward achieving your vision of seamless remote efficiency.

In the digital age, where the globe is your office and the internet your marketplace, mastering SEO Basics for Remote Business Visibility is not just an advantage—it's a necessity. Imagine navigating the vast ocean of online content without a compass; that's a business without SEO. Now, let's dive into the heart of your concerns, armed with humor and devoid of jargon, to explore how SEO can be the beacon for your remote business.

Why is SEO crucial for remote businesses, and how does it differ from traditional SEO? First off, remote businesses face the unique challenge of standing out in a digital landscape without a physical footprint. Traditional SEO strategies focus on drawing traffic through generic keywords and backlinks. However, for remote businesses, it's about crafting a niche online presence that not only reaches a global audience but also resonates with local searches, thanks to the magic of local SEO. It's about being everywhere, yet nowhere, all at once. Imagine telling Google, "Hey, we're based in nowhere land, but we can serve customers from everywhere land." That's the power of tailored SEO strategies for remote businesses.

How can remote businesses leverage local

SEO despite their global reach? It sounds like a paradox, doesn't it? A business without borders focusing on local SEO. Yet, it's about signaling to search engines that you're relevant to local audiences, even if your team is spread across time zones. Utilizing local keywords, creating location-specific pages, and claiming your Google My Business listing (even if it's a virtual office) can enhance your visibility to a local audience. It's like throwing a wide net with small, precise holes—you catch exactly what you're aiming for without limiting your reach.

What are the must-have SEO tools and strategies for remote businesses looking to enhance their online visibility? Beyond the well-trodden path of Google Analytics and SEMrush, remote businesses should explore tools like Moz Local for boosting local SEO presence and Ahrefs for deep-diving into niche keywords that match their unique offerings. But it's not just about the tools; it's about crafting content that speaks the language of your audience, using blog posts, videos, and social media to create a narrative that search engines love to share. It's about being so specific in your SEO efforts that even the most niche audience feels like you're speaking directly to them.

Remember that SEO is not a one-size-fits-all solution but a tailored suit that should fit the unique contours of your remote business. The journey to SEO mastery is ongoing, a blend of art, science, and a dash of creativity. So, keep experimenting, keep learning, and let your business shine in the digital expanse, one search query at a time.

In the realm of remote work, the art of professional communication is not just a skill—it's the very lifeline that connects dispersed teams across the digital divide. As we delve into the intricacies of **Professional Communication in a Remote Setting**, it's essential to address the pressing concerns that might be swirling in your mind. After all, in an era where emojis can be considered a form of feedback and virtual meetings are the new boardrooms, navigating the nuances of digital dialogue is more crucial than ever.

Establishing Clear Communication Norms

The first hurdle many remote teams face is the lack of clear communication norms. Without the non-verbal cues and spontaneous conversations that come naturally in an office setting, remote teams need a solid framework to ensure clarity and prevent misunderstandings. Establishing guidelines on response times, preferred communication channels, and meeting etiquettes can set the stage for seamless interactions. Tools like **Slack** for instant messaging and **Asana** for task management can help create a structured environment where expectations are clear, and everyone is on the same page.

Choosing the Right Tools for Your Team

With a plethora of digital tools at our disposal, selecting the ones that best fit your team's needs can be daunting. The key is to focus on tools that enhance collaboration without adding unnecessary complexity. For instance, **Zoom** has become synonymous with video conferencing, offering features like breakout rooms and virtual backgrounds that cater to various remote work scenarios. However, lesser-known tools like **Loom** for asynchronous video messages or **Mural** for visual collaboration can offer unique advantages, depending on your team's specific needs.

Fostering a Culture of Open Communication

The backbone of effective remote communication is not just the tools but the culture that surrounds them. Encouraging an environment where feedback is welcomed, and every voice is heard can significantly impact your team's morale and productivity. Regular check-ins, virtual coffee breaks, and dedicated channels for non-work-related chat can help build a sense of community and belonging. Platforms like **Donut** within Slack can randomly pair team members for virtual meetups, breaking down silos and promoting a more cohesive team dynamic.

Beyond the Basics

While tools and platforms form the foundation of remote communication, the essence lies in how these tools are utilized to foster genuine connections. It's about creating a space where team members feel valued and heard, transcending geographical boundaries to build a unified team spirit.

As we wrap up this exploration of **Professional Communication in a Remote Setting**, remember that the journey doesn't end here. The landscape of digital tools and communication strategies is ever-evolving, and staying adaptable is key. Perhaps the next frontier in remote communication lies in leveraging AI-driven analytics to personalize interaction strategies or exploring virtual reality meetings for a more immersive experience. The possibilities are endless, and the future of remote work communication is as exciting as it is unpredictable.

Let your guiding principle be a commitment to clarity, empathy, and innovation. By doing so, you'll not only enhance your team's efficiency and cohesion but also pave the way for a more connected and collaborative remote work culture.

————

EMBRACE THE DIGITAL FIRST IMPRESSION: Recognize the paramount importance of a 'remote-friendly' website. Your digital storefront should be more than aesthetically pleasing—it must be a versatile tool that facilitates real-time communication, intuitive navigation, and adapts flawlessly across devices.

Engage and Retain Your Audience: Content reigns supreme in the digital domain. Cultivate a rich repository of interactive content—blogs, videos, and customer testimonials—that not only tells your brand's story but also fosters trust and credibility.

Transform Browsers into Buyers: Integrate e-commerce functionalities and secure payment gateways into your website. Clear calls-to-action (CTAs) should guide visitors effortlessly from exploration to transaction, making every click a potential conversion.

Select Your Digital Arsenal Wisely: The digital tools you choose are the lifelines of your remote operations. Opt for tools that enhance team communication, collaboration, and productivity. Consider ease of use, integration capabilities, scalability, and security features as your criteria for selection.

Explore Beyond the Conventional: Venture into the realm of lesser-known digital tools that offer unique advantages for your specific business needs. Tools like Asana for project management, Notion for an all-in-one workspace, and Miro for collaborative brainstorming can unlock new levels of efficiency and innovation.

Master the Art of SEO: Tailor your SEO strategies to ensure your business stands out in a digital landscape devoid of physical footprints. Leverage local SEO, even as a borderless business, to enhance visibility to local audiences through strategic use of local keywords and creating location-specific pages.

Cultivate a Culture of Open Communication: Establish clear communication norms and choose digital platforms that foster a sense of community and belonging among your team. Encourage feedback, schedule regular check-ins, and promote informal interactions to build a cohesive remote work culture.

Stay Agile and Adaptable: The digital landscape is perpetually evolving. Stay informed about the latest tools, trends, and strategies. Be ready to pivot your approaches and experiment with new technologies to maintain a competitive edge.

Commit to Continuous Learning: The path to digital mastery is ongoing. Embrace the blend of art, science, and creativity that SEO and digital marketing demand. Keep experimenting, keep learning, and let your business shine brighter with each search query.

Forge Ahead with Clarity and Empathy: Let these principles guide your remote communication strategies. As you explore new frontiers in digital interaction, from AI-driven analytics to virtual reality meetings, remember that at the heart of technology lies the power to connect us more deeply.

content creation and management for remote teams

. . .

IMAGINE launching into the cosmos of digital content without a spaceship. That's pretty much what diving into **Remote Content Strategy Development** without a plan feels like. You're out there, floating in the vastness of the internet, hoping your message somehow lands on the right planet—or, in this case, your target audience. This isn't just about hurling content into the digital void and crossing your fingers. It's about crafting a narrative that not only supports your remote work culture and business goals but also engages your audience in a way that feels as personal as getting a DM from your favorite meme account.

Planning content that supports remote work culture and business goals isn't about ticking boxes on a content calendar. It's about creating a blueprint for a digital ecosystem where your content acts as the gravity that pulls your audience into orbit around your brand. Think of it as building your own Death Star of content strategy—minus the whole blowing up planets part, of course.

When it comes to **engaging remote audiences with targeted content**, the secret sauce is authenticity mixed with a dash of creativity. It's like being at a party and finding someone who's as obsessed with your niche hobby as you are. That instant connection is what you're aiming for, but on a scale that spans continents and time zones.

Content Creation and Management for Remote Teams turns the spotlight on the unsung heroes behind the screen. These digital nomads and home office warriors are the ones turning coffee into content, one sip at a time. But here's the kicker: managing a remote content team requires more than just a shared Google Drive and a weekly Zoom call. It's about fostering a culture where creativity flourishes, deadlines are met with enthusiasm rather than dread, and everyone's on the same page—even if that page is a virtual one.

Boldly stating your goals and boldly mapping out your content strategy ensures that your team is not just shooting stars passing in the night. It's about aligning your content with the celestial bodies of your business objectives, ensuring every piece of content, from blog posts to tweets, moves you closer to your mission.

Quotes from content strategy luminaries like Ann Handley or Joe Pulizzi might as well be your North Star, guiding you through the nebula of digital marketing. They remind us that "Content is king, but engagement is queen, and the lady rules the house!" It's not just about what you say; it's about how you say it and ensuring it resonates with your audience on a human level.

Incorporating real-world examples from brands that have mastered the art of remote content strategy can serve as your Apollo missions—proof that not only can it be done, but it can be done with style. Whether it's a small startup that's built a loyal community through authentic storytelling or a global brand that's mastered the art of digital engagement, these examples provide the blueprint for what's possible.

The digital landscape is your playground, and with the right strategy, team, and execution, there's no limit to the worlds you can conquer. So, strap in, fire up your content engines, and let's make this journey legendary. Remember, in the vast expanse of the internet, your content is the beacon that guides your audience home.

This isn't about slapping together a few blog posts or social media updates; it's about orchestrating a symphony of content that resonates across the cosmos of the internet, all while your team members float in their own little space pods, tethered together by Wi-Fi signals.

Collaborative content creation in a remote environment throws out the old playbook. Gone are the days of brainstorming sessions in glass-walled conference rooms. Now, it's about harnessing the collective brainpower of your team, scattered across time zones, in a way that feels as close-knit as a campfire storytelling session. Tools like **Trello** and **Asana** have become the digital campfires around which we gather, sharing ideas and forging connections in the ether of cyberspace.

When it comes to **tools and techniques for remote content production**, we're not just talking about your garden-variety word processors and email. Oh no, we're venturing into the realm of **Notion** for all-in-one workspace magic, **Slack** for real-time banter that fuels creativity, and **Zoom** for when you need to look into the whites of your team's eyes and say, "We're hitting 'publish' on this masterpiece at dawn."

But let's address the three-headed Cerberus lurking in the shadows of this star-studded journey:

- **How do we keep the creative juices flowing when we're not even in the**

same zip code? It's about creating a culture where ideas are free to roam wild, supported by tools like **Miro**, a digital whiteboard that turns remote collaboration into an art form. Picture this: your team's ideas, sprawling across a virtual canvas, growing and intertwining like vines in a lush, digital jungle.

- **What's the best way to ensure our content hits the mark, every time, without the luxury of in-person feedback?** Enter **ContentCal** and **BuzzSumo**, the dynamic duo of content planning and performance tracking. They're like the droids you've been looking for, analyzing the digital landscape to ensure your content not only lands but sticks the landing.

- **How do we pivot when the digital winds change direction?** Flexibility is the name of the game, and tools like **Google Analytics** and **SEMrush** are your navigational charts. They help you read the stars, understand the trends, and adjust your sails accordingly, ensuring your content strategy remains as agile as a cat in zero gravity.

As we orbit back to **Content Creation and Management for Remote Teams**, let's not forget that this journey is about more than just the tools and tactics. It's about building a constellation of content that guides your audience through the digital night sky. It's about stories that resonate, information that enlightens, and a brand voice that echoes across the void, connecting with hearts and minds across the globe.

In the grand finale of this cosmic opera, remember: the digital landscape is ever-expanding, filled with both challenges and opportunities. But with the right crew, a map of the stars, and a dash of daring, there's no limit to the worlds you can explore and the audiences you can captivate. So, buckle up, content creators. It's time to take the helm and steer your brand into the uncharted territories of the digital universe, where your next great adventure awaits.

Navigating the digital seas of **Content Management Systems for Remote Operations** is akin to captaining a ship through uncharted waters. It's thrilling, a tad daunting, but oh-so-crucial for any digital explorer aiming to conquer the vast online universe. This journey isn't just about hoisting sails (or, in our case, hitting 'upload'); it's about ensuring your vessel is equipped with the most advanced navigation systems to keep your content treasure trove accessible, organized, and, most importantly, shareable across the seven digital seas.

Utilizing CMS platforms that support remote access and collaboration is the modern-day equivalent of having a map where 'X' marks the spot. Except, in this scenario, 'X' represents your content's ability to reach the right audience at the right time, without the need for your crew to be huddled together on the same deck. Imagine platforms like **WordPress**, **Drupal**, or **Joomla** as your ship, each offering different capabilities, from the speed of deployment to the robustness of customization, ensuring that no matter where your crew is, the content ship sails smoothly.

When charting the course for **best practices for managing content workflows remotely**, it's crucial to have a compass pointing towards efficiency, collaboration, and adaptability. Tools like **Trello**, **Asana**, and **Monday.com** become the stars by which you navigate, allowing your team to plot the content journey from ideation to publication, all while keeping the dreaded sea monsters of miscommunication and deadline drift at bay.

But let's tackle the three sirens luring many a content team onto the rocks:

- **How do we ensure seamless collaboration across different time zones?** The answer lies in choosing a CMS that's as flexible as it is powerful. **Confluence** by Atlassian, for instance, not only allows for real-time collaboration but also integrates with **Jira**, making it a formidable ally in keeping your content voyage on course, no matter where your crew is anchored.

- **What's the secret to keeping our content strategy aligned with our business goals, especially when our team is scattered across the globe?** Enter **ContentCal**, a platform that not only allows for meticulous planning and scheduling but also offers analytics to ensure your content hits the mark. It's like having a lookout in the crow's nest, ensuring your content strategy doesn't veer off course.

- **How can we pivot our content strategy based on real-time feedback and analytics without causing chaos on deck?** The magic lies in leveraging tools like **Google Analytics** and **SEMrush**, which offer insights as deep as the Mariana Trench. These tools allow you to monitor your content's performance in real-time, making it easier to adjust your sails before the wind changes.

As we delve deeper into **Content Creation and Management for Remote Teams**, remember, this odyssey is more than just about the tools and tactics. It's about creating a digital ecosystem where your content thrives, engaging your audience in a way that feels as personal as a message in a bottle found on a distant shore.

In the grand tapestry of the digital cosmos, **Content Management Systems for Remote Operations** are not just about maintaining order amidst chaos; they're about charting a course towards unexplored territories, where your content can shine like a beacon, guiding your audience back to you, time and again.

So, grab your compass, set your sights on the horizon, and let's embark on this adventure together. Remember, in the vast expanse of the digital ocean, your CMS is the ship that carries your content treasures. Choose wisely, captain well, and the digital world is yours to explore.

When **Integrating SEO with Remote Content**, it's essential to grasp the significance of enhancing remote content visibility through SEO and the strategies for keyword optimization in a remote work context. This understanding is crucial for anyone looking to elevate their online presence and ensure their content reaches the intended audience effectively.

Addressing Key Concerns:

- **Enhancing Remote Content Visibility Through SEO:** The importance of SEO in remote content creation cannot be overstated. It ensures that content is not only created but seen and engaged with by the target audience. Utilizing SEO tools like Google Analytics for web traffic analysis and SEMrush for advanced SEO strategies can significantly improve content visibility.

- **Strategies for Keyword Optimization in a Remote Work Context:** Keyword optimization is pivotal for SEO success. Tools such as Ahrefs and Moz offer insights into keyword performance and competition, enabling remote teams to target their content more effectively.

- **Utilizing CMS Platforms That Support Remote Access and Collaboration:** Content Management

Systems (CMS) like WordPress, Drupal, and Joomla are essential for remote operations, allowing for seamless access and collaboration across teams. These platforms ensure that content management and SEO optimization efforts are cohesive and efficient.

Introducing Novel Tools and Resources:

While familiar tools like Google Analytics and SEMrush are foundational, exploring lesser-known resources can offer unique advantages. For instance, exploring niche forums or industry-specific databases can provide insider knowledge and networking opportunities that are invaluable for SEO and content strategy.

- **Regular SEO Audits:** Conducting regular SEO audits using tools like SEMrush can identify areas for improvement and help maintain an optimized online presence.
- **Collaborative Keyword Research:** Utilizing platforms like Slack for team communication enables a collaborative

approach to keyword research and strategy development.

- **Content Calendar Planning:** Tools like ContentCal facilitate the planning and scheduling of SEO-optimized content, ensuring a consistent and strategic approach to content publication.

Integrating SEO with remote content creation and management is not just about using the right tools; it's about adopting a strategic approach that aligns with your business goals and audience needs. By focusing on enhancing content visibility through SEO and employing effective keyword optimization strategies, remote teams can achieve greater engagement and success in the digital landscape. The exploration of both well-known and lesser-known tools and resources is essential for staying competitive and innovative in SEO practices.

social media and community building remotely

. . .

IN THE DIGITAL AGE, where remote work is becoming the norm, mastering the art of choosing the right platforms to reach and engage your audience is more crucial than ever. This chapter is dedicated to guiding you through the process of identifying the best social media channels for remote work enthusiasts and clients, and tailoring your strategies to foster a remote-first community effectively.

Identifying the Right Social Media Channels: Your journey begins with pinpointing which platforms your target audience prefers. It's not about spreading yourself thin across every available channel but focusing on those where your audience actively engages. This strategic selection ensures that your efforts resonate with the right people, amplifying your message's reach and impact.

Tailoring Your Strategy for Each Platform: With your platforms chosen, the next step is to customize your approach for each one. Different platforms cater to different user behaviors and content preferences, necessitating a nuanced strategy that speaks directly to the audience on each channel. This tailored approach is essential for creating meaningful connections and fostering engagement.

Engaging Your Remote Audience: True engagement goes beyond posting content; it's about sparking conversations and building a community. This chapter offers strategies to encourage interaction, making your audience feel heard and valued. It's about transforming followers into active community members who contribute to and advocate for your brand.

Leveraging Analytics to Refine Your Approach: To stay ahead, you'll need to embrace analytics. Understanding how your content performs and how users interact with it allows you to make informed decisions, fine-tuning your strategy to ensure it remains effective and resonant with your audience.

Learning from the Best: Gain insights from industry leaders who have successfully engaged remote audiences. This chapter distills their best practices into actionable strategies you can apply, from content personalization to community management, ensuring you're equipped with the knowledge to thrive in the remote digital landscape.

Applying What You Learn: Through real-world examples and case studies, you'll see these strategies in action. This practical application helps bridge the gap between theory and practice, providing a clearer path for you to implement these tactics in your own remote engagement efforts.

Remember that selecting the right platforms and crafting thoughtful, audience-specific strategies are key to building a successful remote community. By focusing on strategic selection, tailored engagement, and ongoing optimization, you'll not only reach your remote audience more effectively but also create a dynamic community that supports and amplifies your brand in the digital realm.

To excel in Social Media Content Planning for Remote Engagement, it's essential to adopt a strategic and methodical approach. This chapter provides actionable tactics and specific instructions to help you effectively reach and engage a remote-first audience.

Identifying Optimal Platforms: Start by identifying which social media platforms your target audience frequents. Conduct research to understand where remote work enthusiasts and clients are most active.

For instance, LinkedIn is ideal for professional engagement, while Instagram may be better for creative visual content.

Developing a Content Calendar: Create a content calendar that accounts for different time zones to ensure maximum reach. Use tools like Google Calendar or Trello to organize and visualize your content schedule. Plan your posts to coincide with peak activity times in the time zones where your audience resides.

Utilizing Scheduling Tools: Leverage scheduling tools like Buffer, Hootsuite, or Sprout Social to automate your post timings. These tools allow you to schedule posts in advance, ensuring consistent engagement without the need to be online 24/7.

Creating Engaging Content: Develop content that resonates with a remote audience. This could include tips for remote work, success stories, or interactive content like polls and quizzes. Ensure your content is varied and aligns with the interests of your audience.

Engagement Strategies: Foster engagement by encouraging comments, shares, and interaction. Respond promptly to comments and messages to build a community feel. Use calls to action in your posts to encourage audience participation.

Analyzing Performance: Regularly analyze your social media performance using the analytics tools provided by the platforms or external tools like Google Analytics. Track metrics such as engagement rates, best-performing content types, and optimal posting times.

Adapting Your Strategy: Based on your analytics, continually refine your content strategy. Experiment with different types of content, posting schedules, and engagement tactics to find what works best for your audience.

Learning from Success Stories: Study successful brands or influencers within the remote work sphere. Note their content strategies, engagement tactics, and audience interactions to glean insights for your own approach.

By implementing these specific tactics, you can develop a robust social media content plan that effectively engages remote audiences, fostering a sense of community and driving meaningful interactions.

Mastering Engagement Techniques for Remote Communities is not just beneficial—it's essential for building and sustaining vibrant online communities. This chapter delves into effective strategies for fostering engagement through virtual events and webinars, offering you a roadmap to captivate and maintain your remote audience's attention.

Building Online Communities: The foundation of a thriving remote community lies in understanding the interests and needs of your audience. Start by identifying common themes or challenges within the remote work sphere and use these as anchors for your community-building efforts. Engage your audience by creating forums or social media groups where they can share experiences, seek advice, and find support.

Strategies for Virtual Events and Webinars: Virtual events and webinars offer a unique opportunity to engage with your community in real-time. Plan these events around topics that resonate with your audience, providing value and fostering a sense of belonging. Utilize platforms like Zoom or Webex for webinars and consider interactive tools like Slido or Mentimeter to encourage participation.

Content Calendars for Global Engagement: When managing a remote community, it's crucial to consider the diverse locations of your members. Develop a content calendar that schedules posts, discussions, and events at times convenient for a global audience. Tools like CoSchedule or Buffer can help you plan and automate this content, ensuring consistent engagement across time zones.

Leveraging Engagement Tools: To keep your community active and engaged, incorporate tools designed for interaction. Use platforms like Discord or Slack for real-time communication, and consider

Trello or Asana for organizing community projects or initiatives. These tools not only facilitate interaction but also help in building a structured, collaborative environment.

Measuring Community Engagement: Understanding the impact of your engagement strategies is key to their success. Utilize analytics tools available on social media platforms or specialized tools like Google Analytics to track participation, engagement rates, and overall community growth. This data will guide you in refining your strategies and ensuring they align with your community's preferences.

Best Practices for Community Engagement: Learn from successful remote communities by observing how they foster interaction and participation. Implement best practices such as regular check-ins, featured member stories, and community challenges to keep your audience engaged and invested in the community.

Actionable Steps for Community Builders: To effectively engage your remote community, start by setting clear objectives for what you want to achieve. Identify the platforms where your community thrives, create a content calendar that caters to global time zones, and regularly evaluate the effectiveness of your engagement strategies. Adapt and evolve your approach based on feedback and analytics to ensure your community remains vibrant and engaged.

Engagement Techniques for Remote Communities are pivotal in creating a sense of connection and belonging among remote individuals. By strategically planning virtual events, tailoring content to a global audience, and leveraging the right tools, you can cultivate a thriving online community that supports and enriches the remote work experience.

Understanding and mastering Performance Monitoring from Afar is crucial for anyone looking to optimize their online presence and ensure their content resonates with their audience. This section delves into the essential tools and metrics for analyzing social media performance remotely and outlines strategies for adjusting your approach based on remote audience feedback.

Tools and Metrics for Remote Performance Analysis: To effectively monitor your social media performance, familiarize yourself with key analytics tools like Google Analytics and platform-specific insights. These tools provide valuable data on user engagement, reach, and interaction, allowing you to gauge the success of your content and identify areas for improvement.

Analyzing Audience Engagement: Pay close attention to metrics such as engagement rates, click-through rates, and audience growth. These indicators will help you understand how well your content is connecting with your audience and which types of posts generate the most interaction.

Utilizing Scheduling and Automation Tools: Tools like Buffer, Hootsuite, or Later are invaluable for managing your social media presence remotely. They allow you to schedule posts in advance, ensuring consistent engagement with your audience, and provide analytics to monitor the performance of your content.

Adjusting Strategies Based on Feedback: Use the insights gained from your analytics to refine your content strategy. If certain types of content are resonating more with your audience, focus on producing more of that content. Conversely, if some strategies are not yielding the desired results, don't hesitate to pivot and try new approaches.

Engagement and Feedback Loops: Establish mechanisms for gathering and analyzing audience feedback. This can include monitoring comments, conducting surveys, or using social listening tools. Understanding your audience's preferences and concerns will enable you to tailor your content more effectively.

Best Practices for Remote Performance Monitoring: Stay updated with the latest trends and tools in social media analytics. Regularly review your performance metrics and be prepared to adapt your strategy to align with your audience's evolving preferences and the dynamic nature of social media.

Actionable Steps for Effective Monitoring: Start by setting clear goals for what you want to achieve with your social media presence. Regularly review your analytics to understand your audience's behavior and preferences. Use this data to inform your content creation, ensuring it aligns with your audience's interests and engagement patterns.

By embracing these strategies and tools for Performance Monitoring from Afar, you can ensure that your social media efforts are not only reaching your target audience but also engaging them in meaningful ways. This proactive approach to monitoring and adjusting your strategy will help you build a stronger, more connected online community, even from a distance.

HERE's a step-by-step summary of the strategies and insights discussed:

IDENTIFYING the Right Social Media Channels:

- Conduct research to determine where your target audience, particularly remote work enthusiasts and clients, is most active.
- Focus your efforts on platforms that align with your audience's preferences to maximize impact and engagement.

Tailoring Your Strategy for Each Platform:

- Customize your approach for each selected platform, considering the unique user behaviors and content preferences.
- Develop a nuanced strategy that resonates with the audience on each channel, fostering meaningful connections.

Creating Engaging Content:

- Develop a content calendar that accommodates global time zones, ensuring your posts reach your audience at optimal times.
- Utilize scheduling tools like Buffer, Hootsuite, or Sprout Social to maintain a consistent online presence.

Fostering Community Engagement:

- Go beyond posting content; encourage conversations and community building.
- Create forums or social media groups where your audience can interact, share experiences, and support each other.

Leveraging Analytics for Strategy Refinement:

- Regularly analyze your social media performance using tools like Google Analytics to understand audience engagement and content effectiveness.
- Adjust your strategies based on analytics insights to keep your approach aligned with audience preferences and behaviors.

Learning from Successful Engagement Practices:

- Study successful brands or influencers within the remote work sphere to glean insights into effective engagement strategies.
- Apply best practices from industry leaders, adapting their successful tactics to your unique context.

Implementing Virtual Events and Webinars:

- Utilize virtual events and webinars to engage with your community in real-time, providing value and fostering a sense of belonging.
- Choose topics that resonate with your audience and use interactive tools to encourage participation.

Monitoring and Adjusting Based on Feedback:

- Establish feedback loops to gather and analyze audience input, using this information to tailor your content and engagement strategies.
- Be adaptable, ready to pivot your approach based on audience feedback and changing digital landscapes.

Actionable Steps for Community Builders:

- Set clear objectives for your digital engagement efforts.

- Regularly evaluate the effectiveness of your strategies, using data and feedback to inform ongoing adjustments.

Future Directions and Continuous Learning:

- Stay informed about the latest trends and tools in digital engagement and social media analytics.
- Continuously refine your approach, embracing innovation and adapting to the evolving needs of your remote audience.

marketing strategies for
remote businesses

. . .

IN THE BUSTLING DIGITAL
MARKETPLACE, mastering Email Marketing in a
Remote Context is not just an option; it's a necessity
for those aiming to connect with remote work enthusiasts and clients globally. This chapter, a crucial part of
"Marketing Strategies for Remote Businesses," offers a
deep dive into building a targeted email list and
personalizing email campaigns to resonate with a
diverse, global remote audience.

**Building an Email List with a Focus on
Remote Work Enthusiasts**: The first step in a
successful email marketing strategy is to build an email
list that specifically targets remote work enthusiasts.
Utilize sign-up forms on your website, social media
channels, and at virtual events to gather email

addresses. Offer valuable incentives like free ebooks, webinars, or exclusive content to encourage sign-ups, ensuring that your list is populated with individuals genuinely interested in remote work.

Personalizing Email Campaigns for a Global Remote Audience: Once you have your email list, the key to engagement is personalization. Use data analytics to segment your audience based on their interests, location, and interaction with your previous emails. This segmentation allows you to tailor your messages, ensuring that they are relevant and engaging to each recipient. Tools like Mailchimp or Constant Contact offer features that enable you to automate this personalization process efficiently.

Utilizing Tools for Effective Email Campaigns: Leverage email marketing tools to design, send, and monitor your campaigns. These tools provide templates, automation, and analytics to refine your strategy over time. A/B testing features can help you determine which email elements (like subject lines or call-to-actions) resonate best with your audience.

Engagement Through Storytelling: Incorporate storytelling into your emails to build a connection with your audience. Share success stories, case studies, or insights that are relatable to remote workers. This approach not only makes your content more engaging but also helps to establish your brand as an authority in the remote work space.

Feedback Loops and Adjustments: Establish a system for collecting feedback from your email recipients. Use surveys, direct replies, or engagement metrics to gather insights into what your audience values. Regularly adjust your email content and strategy based on this feedback to ensure continuous improvement and relevance.

Conclusion and Continuous Learning: Conclude each email campaign with a clear call to action, guiding your readers on what to do next. Always be in the loop of evolving email marketing trends and best practices to keep your strategies fresh and effective.

In today's interconnected world, where remote work is not just a trend but a mainstay, the art of Leveraging Partnerships for Remote Reach stands as a pivotal strategy for businesses aiming to expand their horizons. This section unravels the essence of forging alliances with remote businesses and influencers, alongside crafting virtual co-marketing campaigns that resonate with a global audience.

Collaborating with Other Remote Businesses and Influencers: The digital landscape offers a fertile ground for collaborations that can amplify your brand's reach. Identifying potential partners who share a similar audience or values can lead to mutually beneficial partnerships. Whether it's a guest blog exchange, a joint webinar, or a co-created product, these collaborations can open new channels for audience engagement and brand exposure.

Strategies for Virtual Co-Marketing Campaigns: Virtual co-marketing campaigns harness the power of partnership in the digital realm, allowing businesses to pool resources, creativity, and audiences. Planning a campaign involves aligning goals, messaging, and metrics to ensure that all parties benefit and contribute equally. Utilizing platforms like Zoom for webinars, Google Drive for collaborative content creation, and social media for cross-promotion can enhance the campaign's reach and effectiveness.

Utilizing Tools for Collaboration and Campaign Management: Effective partnership and campaign management require the right tools. Platforms like Slack for communication, Trello for project management, and Hootsuite for social media coordination can streamline the collaborative process, ensuring all stakeholders are aligned and informed.

Engagement Through Shared Storytelling: A compelling narrative that intertwines the strengths and stories of all partners can captivate the audience more deeply than isolated efforts. Shared storytelling not only enhances the campaign's appeal but also builds a stronger connection with the audience, fostering a sense of community and shared values.

Feedback Loops and Data-Driven Adjustments: Establishing mechanisms to gather feedback and measure the success of partnership campaigns is crucial. Tools like Google Analytics and social media insights provide valuable data to assess performance and guide future strategies. Regularly reviewing these metrics allows businesses to refine their approach, ensuring that partnerships continue to yield beneficial results.

The journey doesn't end here; it's an ongoing process of exploration, collaboration, and adaptation. By embracing the strategies outlined, businesses can navigate the remote landscape with agility, forging partnerships that transcend geographical boundaries and create lasting impacts.

In essence, Leveraging Partnerships for Remote Reach is more than a strategy; it's a dynamic approach to business growth in the digital age. By understanding the nuances of remote collaborations and virtual co-marketing, businesses can unlock new opportunities, foster innovation, and build a resilient brand that thrives in the ever-evolving remote work ecosystem.

Advanced Content Marketing for Remote Engagement emerges as a cornerstone for businesses aiming to establish trust and authority. This chapter delves into the strategic use of content marketing to captivate and maintain the attention of remote work enthusiasts, offering a blueprint for success in this niche.

Building Trust and Authority Through Content Marketing: At the heart of effective content marketing lies the ability to build trust and establish authority within the remote work community. This involves creating valuable, insightful content that addresses the needs, challenges, and interests of remote workers. By consistently delivering high-quality content, businesses can position themselves as thought leaders in the remote work space, fostering a loyal and engaged audience.

Case Studies of Successful Content Marketing by Remote Companies: Learning from the success stories of remote companies that have excelled in content marketing provides invaluable insights. These case studies highlight the strategies, tactics, and types of content that have resonated with remote audiences, offering a roadmap for other businesses to replicate and adapt these successes to their unique contexts.

Utilizing Tools and Resources for Content Creation and Distribution: Leveraging the right tools and resources is crucial for efficient and effective content marketing. Platforms like WordPress for blog publishing, Canva for graphic design, and Buffer for social media management enable businesses to create, distribute, and monitor their content seamlessly. These tools not only streamline the content marketing process but also provide analytics to gauge performance and engagement.

Engaging Remote Work Enthusiasts with Relevant Content: To truly engage a remote audience, content must be relevant, relatable, and valuable. This means understanding the audience's preferences, pain points, and interests. Surveys, social media interactions, and audience analytics can provide valuable insights into what content will resonate most, allowing businesses to tailor their content strategy accordingly.

Strategies for Virtual Co-Marketing Campaigns: Collaborating with other businesses or influencers in the remote work niche can amplify content reach and impact. Virtual co-marketing campaigns, whether through joint webinars, co-authored guides, or shared social media initiatives, can introduce businesses to new audiences and add diverse perspectives to their content offerings.

Feedback Loops and Continuous Improvement: Establishing feedback mechanisms is vital for refining content marketing strategies. Encouraging comments, conducting audience surveys, and monitoring engagement metrics can provide direct insights into what content is most effective and what areas need adjustment. This continuous loop of feedback and improvement ensures that content marketing efforts remain aligned with audience needs and preferences.

Paid Advertising Basics for Targeting Remote Audiences is crucial for businesses looking to effectively reach and engage this growing demographic. This segment delves into the strategies and tools necessary to navigate the paid advertising landscape, ensuring your message resonates with remote workers and clients worldwide.

Exploring Effective Paid Channels for Remote Audiences: Identifying the right channels is the first step in crafting a successful paid advertising strategy. Platforms like LinkedIn, known for its professional network, and Facebook, with its extensive targeting options, offer valuable opportunities to reach remote work enthusiasts. It's essential to evaluate each platform's potential to connect with your specific audience, considering factors like user demographics, behavior, and preferences.

Tailoring Ad Campaigns for Diverse Remote Work Communities: The diversity within remote work communities necessitates a tailored approach to advertising. Segmenting your audience based on factors such as job roles, industries, and interests allows for more personalized and relevant ad campaigns. Utilizing tools like Google Ads' targeting features or Facebook's Custom Audiences can help refine your strategy, ensuring your ads reach the most receptive viewers.

Leveraging Analytics for Insightful Campaign Adjustments: To maximize the effectiveness of your paid advertising efforts, it's vital to leverage analytics. Platforms offer various metrics to track the performance of your ads, providing insights into aspects like click-through rates, conversion rates, and audience engagement. Regularly analyzing this data helps in making informed decisions to optimize your campaigns, adjust targeting, and improve overall ROI.

Engagement Strategies for Remote Audiences: Engaging remote audiences through paid advertising involves more than just capturing their attention. It's about creating value and fostering connections. Incorporate clear calls to action, offer valuable resources or solutions, and ensure your ad content aligns with the interests and needs of remote workers. Interactive formats, such as webinars or live Q&A sessions, can also enhance engagement and build a sense of community.

Case Studies of Successful Campaigns: Learning from successful paid advertising campaigns targeting remote audiences can provide valuable lessons. Analyze case studies to understand the strategies, messaging, and creative approaches that resonated with remote workers. These insights can inspire your campaigns, helping you to craft messages that not only reach but also genuinely connect with your target audience.

Continuous Learning and Adaptation: The landscape of paid advertising is ever-evolving, with new platforms, tools, and strategies emerging regularly. Staying informed about the latest trends and best practices is essential for maintaining the effectiveness of your campaigns. Attend webinars, follow industry leaders, and participate in forums dedicated to digital marketing to keep your knowledge up-to-date.

In conclusion, mastering Paid Advertising Basics for Targeting Remote Audiences is a dynamic and ongoing process. By choosing the right channels, tailoring your campaigns, leveraging analytics, and continuously learning, you can effectively reach and engage the burgeoning remote work community. This not only enhances your brand's visibility but also contributes to building lasting relationships with a global audience, positioning your business as a key player in the remote work ecosystem.

conclusion

. . .

IN THIS COMPREHENSIVE GUIDE, we've journeyed through the multifaceted landscape of establishing and nurturing a remote business, from laying the foundational vision to executing sophisticated marketing strategies. Each chapter has been meticulously crafted to equip you with the knowledge, tools, and insights necessary to thrive in the digital-first world, where remote work is not just a trend but a mainstay of the modern business environment.

Chapter 1 set the stage by encouraging you to embrace your remote business vision, highlighting the scalability and flexibility that come with operating digitally. Through success stories and strategic market understanding, we've underscored the importance of setting SMART goals and effectively planning resources in a virtual setting, ensuring your remote venture is built on a solid foundation.

Chapter 2 delved into the essence of building a remote brand identity, emphasizing the power of story-telling and the significance of a strong visual and communicative online presence. We explored how to maintain brand consistency across digital platforms, ensuring your message resonates with a global audience.

Chapter 3 focused on the critical aspects of online presence and the selection of digital tools that enhance remote work efficiency. From website essentials to SEO basics, this chapter provided a roadmap for establishing a robust digital footprint and fostering professional communication within remote teams.

Chapter 4 addressed the core of content creation and management, offering strategies for developing engaging content that aligns with your remote work culture and business objectives. We examined collabo-rative content production and the effective use of content management systems, integrating SEO to maximize your remote content's visibility.

Chapter 5 shifted the spotlight to social media and community building, guiding you through the process of selecting the right platforms and crafting content that caters to a remote-first audience. We shared techniques for nurturing online communities and monitoring social media performance to refine your engagement strategies continually.

Chapter 6 rounded out the guide with a deep dive into marketing strategies tailored for remote businesses. From the nuances of email marketing to the dynamics of partnerships and content marketing, this chapter provided a blueprint for leveraging various marketing channels to connect with remote workers and clients effectively.

As we conclude this guide, remember that the journey of running a remote business is one of continuous learning and adaptation. The digital landscape is ever-evolving, and staying attuned to the latest trends, technologies, and best practices is crucial for sustained success. Embrace the flexibility, innovation, and global reach that remote work offers, and let the strategies and insights shared in this book be your compass as you navigate the exciting world of remote business.

Your venture into the realm of remote business is not just a path to success—it's a contribution to a broader movement that's reshaping the way we work and interact. Armed with the knowledge from this guide, you're now equipped to build a remote business that not only achieves its goals but also fosters a sense of community, innovation, and inclusivity in the digital age.

BEFORE STARTING YOUR BUSINESS!

- CHOOSING A BUSINESS STRUCTURE
- REGISTERING A BUSINESS NAME
- BUSINESS TAX ID & LICENSES
- SETTING UP BUSINESS FINANCES
- GETTING BUSINESS INSURANCE
- PRODUCT DEVELOPMENT STRATEGIES
- MARKETING PLAN FOR STARTUPS
- SALES STRATEGIES FOR NEW BUSINESSES

HOW TO START YOUR
BUSINESS

Entrepreneurs Guide to Launching
Your Startup with Effective
Business Planning Strategies

HUNTER HAZELTON

www.ingramcontent.com/pod-product-compliance
Lightning Source LLC
Chambersburg PA
CBHW071100290526
45795CB00004B/1579